Strength

For Each Day

30-Days of Daily Devotion

By: Yolanda M. Simmons

Strength

For Each Day

30-Days of Daily Devotion

By: Yolanda M. Simmons

Strength for Each Day

30-Day Daily Devotional

Copyright ©2023 Yolanda M. Simmons

Published by Never A-Mis
Enterprises, LLC
P.O. Box 2298
Byron, GA 31008-2298
www.neveramisenterprises.com

ISBN: 9798985059779

*Printed in the
United States of America*

DEDICATION

I would like to dedicate this book to my mom, Annie Johnson. She has been my biggest and greatest support since day one. She has inspired me to keep pushing, even when I wanted to give up. She has been an example of totally selling out to The Lord. "Thank you, mom!"

I would like to thank my husband John, and my kids, Sequanna and Shakira for giving me their honest opinions and keeping me levelheaded throughout this

entire process. I love you all dearly.

TABLE OF CONTENTS

TABLE OF CONTENTS

TABLE OF CONTENTS

TABLE OF CONTENTS

TABLE OF CONTENTS

TABLE OF CONTENTS

DAY 1
The desires of our hearts.

"Take delight in the Lord, and He will
give you the desires of your heart"
Psalm 37:4 *NLT*

What is your deepest desire (s)? What are you doing to achieve it (them)? In this Scripture God plainly tells us He will give us our deepest and most heartfelt desire (s) if we delight in Him.

All we do should be to please Him; and Only Him. We please Him by following the instructions in the Bible; building an intimate relationship; and having compassion for all people.

In order to get specific instructions from Him, we have to fast and pray.

We will be able to walk according to His will, and not ours.

PRAYER

"Lord help us stay on track with Your will. Give us the desires of our hearts as it is according to Your will. In Jesus name. Amen."

DAY 2
It shall be given.

"Keep on asking and you will receive
what you ask for. Keep on seeking and
you will find. Keep on knocking and
the door will be opened to you"
Matthew 7:7 *NLT*

As kids, when we wanted something, we would ask and beg until we got it (some cases we were threatened not to ask again). Our Father in heaven is waiting for us to ask. We don't have to beg, bater, steal; just simply ask in faith. God already knows what we need. He is waiting for us to ask, then He will move according to our faith.

PRAYER

"Dear Lord, we are confident You will move in our behalf because we are asking in faith. While we wait, we will

worship and pray with great

expectation. In Jesus name, Amen."

DAY 3
Write the vision. Make it plain.

"Then the Lord answered me and said: Write the Vision and make it plain on the tablets that he may run who read it." Habakkuk 2:2 *NIV*

We all have visions, dreams, and goals. The Word of God says to write them down so they are continually before us a constant reminder. When we write them down, it is no longer a thought.

Once we have written it down, we need to post it in place we will be able to see it daily. No matter what life may throw our way because we have written the vision; made it plain, and posted as a reminder, it will surely come to pass.

PRAYER

"Lord, we have done what You declared in Your Word. Lead, guide, and direct us so we may see the manifestation of our visions, dreams, and goals. In Jesus name. Amen"

DAY 4
Faith over Fear.

"Have I not commanded you? Be
strong and courageous. Do not be
frightened and do not be dismayed, for
the Lord your God is with you
wherever you go." Joshua 1:9 *NIV*

"Faith over fear" was the trending quote of the decade, especially when Covid-19 hit the scene. People were weary, worn, and afraid. Hearing or grasping hold to something that would awaken hope was very necessary. The Word of God was trending even though things seemed shaky. Faith over fear is a variation of God's Word.

The Word of God reminded us to stand on The Word of God in the face of fear and adversity.

PRAYER

"Lord, thank You for the reminder that we can stand on Your Word no matter what we have to face. Thank You for the strength to be strong. In Jesus name. Amen."

DAY 5
What you can't see.

"When He had thus spoken, He spat on the ground, and made clay of the spittle, and He anointed the eyes of the blind man with the clay, and He said unto him, go, wash in the pool of Siloam. He went his way therefore and washed and came seeing."
John 9:6-7 *KJV*

The blind man did not have a name. His issue was more important than his name because it would be used to disrupt that fabric of his family and the people who knew his situation. When Jesus called him, everybody already assumed someone sinned in his family.

His issue was a set-up so God could be glorified. Sometimes what we can't see is what will cause us to see!

PRAYER

"Lord help us to trust You when we can't see You or trace You. In Jesus name. Amen"

DAY 6
Broken; but put back together.

"He heals the broken in heart, and
binds up their wounds."
Psalms 147:3 *NIV*

We have all experienced some hurt, disappointment, or heartbreak because it is a part of life. If we don't allow those wounds to heal, they can and will change the direction of our lives away from God.

All throughout the Bible there are stories of those who have experienced the same or greater degrees of hurt, disappointment, or heartbreak, but they overcame because they trusted God to heal them. We have to seek God because He is the Ultimate Healer.

PRAYER

"Dear Lord, help us to trust You enough to give You access to the places we are hurting so You can bind up our wounds. Lord, give us Your peace while we go through the healing process. In Jesus name. Amen"

DAY 7
Walk it out.

"Inside the city, near the Sheep Gate, was the pool of Bethesda, with five covered porches." John 5:2 *NLT*

As Jesus returned to Jerusalem, there was a crowd of people at the pool of Bethesda. Among all the sick, Jesus noticed a man that was lame. Once Jesus saw the lame man looked up, He told him, "Stand up; pick-up your mat, and walk!"

The SAME power Jesus had is STILL available to us today. We have to believe and have faith. Even if we can't see or feel evidence of the healing, continue to walk it out by faith until the manifestation shows up.

PRAYER

"Lord thank You for healing me!

Thank You for the strength to walk out

my process of healing to see

manifestations! In Jesus name. Amen."

DAY 8

In the fire, but not burned.

"Then Nebuchadnezzar came near to the mouth of the burning fiery furnace, and spake, and said, Shadrach, Meshach, and Abednego, ye servants of the Most High God, come forth, and come hither. Then Shadrach, Meshach, and Abednego, came forth of the midst of the fire." Daniel 3:24~26 *KJV*

Daniel's friends were put in the fiery furnace because they would not bow to worship and idol or man. They knew Who's they were, so bowing to another god or idol other than our True and Living God could be worse than the fiery furnace they were facing.

Shadrach, Meshach, and Abednego trusted God in Who God said He was, and what He said He could do. Their complete trust in Him opened up a place for Him to be in the fire with them! When King Nebuchadnezzar looked in, he saw four people instead of three. When the king called them out of the fire, they didn't smell like smoke and there wasn't a hair on them burned!

PRAYER

"Lord help us to stand firm on Your Word no matter what comes our way. Help us to see the way of escape when temptation is all around us. In Jesus name. Amen."

DAY 9
Don't look back.

"And when the morning arose, the
angels hastened Lot, saying, Arise, take
thy wife, and thy two daughters, which
are here; lest thou be consumed in the
iniquity of the city."
Genesis 19:15-16 *KJV*

In the book of Genesis, God was destroying Sodom and Gomorrah by fire after they continued to commit gross sins. Lot and his family were told to run for their lives. He told his wife to run with their daughters, and not to look back. When Lot's wife looked back, she turned into a pillar of salt!

Most of us would have looked back because we are comfortable with what we left behind, and we fear what is ahead because it is unfamiliar. If you have been freed or delivered from your past, don't look back to check on it!

In life we have all done things we were told not to do, and it caused great turmoil. The punishment wasn't our lives, but the wrath of God is brutal. It is in our best interest to do what God tells us to do.

PRAYER

"Dear Lord, we know that obedience is better than sacrifice. Help us to continue to listen to Your instructions, and willfully obey them. In Jesus

name. Amen."

DAY 10

Forbidden fruit.

"The woman was convinced. She saw
that the tree was beautiful, and its fruit
looked delicious, and she wanted the
wisdom it would give her. So, she took
some of the fruit and ate it. Then she
gave some to her husband, who was
with her, and he ate it, too."
Genesis 3:6 *NLT*

The story of Eve being deceived by the serpent is a very familiar. Eve involved Adam, which caused him to sin. Deception causes disobedience to seem like obedience.

As a child we are told not to touch the stove or iron because it is hot. How many times were we told not to touch before we actually touch it? When God tells us not to do something, and we do it anyway, there are consequences we have to deal with, in addition to being burned by the "hot stove or iron".

PRAYER

"Father, God help us do Your will and
block out the distractions around us that
lead us to do the devil's work. In Jesus
name. Amen."

DAY 11
Mastering right thoughts.

"For as he thinks in his heart, so is he.
Eat and drink! He says to you, But his
heart is not with you."
Proverbs 23:7 *NKJV*

Did you know the thoughts in your mind will eventually become actions or reality? As a man thinks, so is he! As an adult, I have learned to allow positive and good thoughts take up space in my mind. Thinking in that manner will lead us to do positive and good things.

I remember growing up we played hide and seek. One person would count, while everybody else ran and hid. Once the person counting was done, they opened their eyes and began to run and look for everyone that was hiding. The counter never doubted whether he was going to find everyone. He knew he was going to find at least one person to tag and make them "IT"! We must have the same positive and good thoughts the counter had in order to get positive results.

PRAYER

"Dear Lord, help us to have good and positive thoughts even when things are not going our way. Help us to be the

"IT" You want us to be. In Jesus name.

Amen."

DAY 12
Peace be still.

"He said, Come. So, Peter got out of the boat and walked on the water and came to Jesus." Matthew 14:29 *ESV*

In Matthew 29, Peter was on the boat with the other disciples preparing to cross over the sea to meet Jesus. A great storm arose, and they became afraid. Then all of sudden they saw someone walking across the water, or a ghost. Jesus began to speak, and they recognized His voice, but they were still afraid. Peter said, "Lord if it is You, tell me to come to You on the water." Jesus said, "Come."

Peter began to walk on the water just as Jesus did. Then the winds started blowing severely, Peter became fearful again, and began sinking, crying out, "Lord save me!" Jesus saved him even though he doubted Him.

Sometimes we get caught up in the moment; our surroundings; even our circumstances and fear rise up. We have to remember the authority we have in Christ and decree ... "Peace Be Still!"

PRAYER

"Dear God, when the storms are raging, teach us how to decree and declare

Peace to be still. In Jesus name.

Amen"

DAY 13

Forgiveness.

"If we confess our sins, He is faith and just to forgive us our sins and to cleanse us from all unrighteousness."
1 John 1:9 *NKJV*

Unforgiveness is a very touchy subject. It is like a disease and can destroy us from the inside out. It consumes and takes away every ounce of joy and peace we have. But God!

God so love the world that He gave ... Because of Jesus, we can forgive. God forgave us insomuch as He gave us Jesus to atone for our sins.

We have to forgive others no matter how bad they may have hurt us. Forgiveness is not for the person who hurt us, it is for US! Call whomever hurt you; tell whoever betrayed you;

call out the name of the person you were holding hostage in your heart and forgive them.

PRAYER

"Dear Lord, go deep within us and reveal and uncover the lingering unforgiveness in us so we can forgive with sincerity. In Jesus name. Amen."

DAY 14
Born to win.

"But thanks be to God, Who gives us the victory through our Lord Jesus Christ." 1 Corinthians 15:57 *NKJV*

I played basketball for one season before I realized it was not my sport at all. I did my best and gave it my all because I don't like to lose. However, sometimes we did lose, and it wasn't a good feeling. Our next game we went harder to make sure we got the win.

Once we taste victory, we want it over and over again. When we accomplish a great task in our lives, we taste victory. Once we experienced defeat, we will do whatever it takes to have the taste of victory on our tongues again. When times get hard don't get overwhelmed, just think about what

victory tastes like!

PRAYER

"Dear God, thank You for helping me

overcome. I am grateful for the victory

and not staying a victim. In Jesus

name. Amen."

DAY 15
Life lessons.

"A good person produces good things
from the treasury of a good heart, and
an evil person produces evil things
from what is in your heart."
Luke 6:45 *NLT*

One thing I have learned in this life is how to walk my own path. I do not try to be like anyone else because I realize when God created me, He broke the mold!

When I was growing up, I would see different girls/women on tv and say I wanted to be like them. As I grew older, I realized the outside may look good, but the inside could be a hot mess! We don't know what Sally or Sam went through to look like they look, or to have what they have.

Live your life. Live with no

regrets. Ask The Lord for what you

need and want. He said ask and it shall

be given. What are you waiting for?

PRAYER

"Dear God, thank You for the

difficulties in my life. Through

troubles my faith has increased and

helped me to learn more. Life lessons

taught me how to depend on You. In

Jesus name. Amen"

DAY 16
From pain to peace.

"We are confident, I say, and would
prefer to be away from the body and at
home with the Lord."
1 Corinthians 5:8 *NIV*

We were born to die. Losing loved ones is a hard pill to swallow. The hurt and pain from losing a loved one can be unbearable sometimes. The pain never leaves, we just learn how to manage and adjust our lives after their gone. Dealing with the pain one day at time, coupled with prayer is the recipe to get through it.

Jesus was our Greatest example. When He left this world, He went back to His original position, on the right side of Our Father. When we lose loved one's who lived according to the Bible, although we miss them; we can have the peace of knowing they are home with The Lord.

PRAYER

"Dear God, when we lose loved ones, please send a gentle reminder to us that they are home, while at the same enveloping us with Your peace. In Jesus name. Amen."

DAY 17
Make room.

"But lift up your rod and stretch out your hand over the sea and divide it. And the children of Israel shall go on dry ground through the midst of the sea." Exodus 14:16 *NKJV*

As Moses led the children of Israel out of Egypt, they were trapped in between Pharoh and his army and the Red Sea in front of them. Moses stretched his hand to the Red Sea, and God miraculously parted it so the children of Israel were able to walk on dry ground to the other side.

The same way God made room for the Israelites He can do it for us today. No matter how big the problem may be, Our God is BIGGER. Give it to God and let Him make room for you.

PRAYER

"Dear Lord, let us depend on You to fix our problems. Help us to take our cares to the altar and leave them there. In Jesus name. Amen."

DAY 18
The power of prayer.

"I tell you, you can pray for anything, and if you believe that you've received it, it will be yours." Mark 11:24 *NLT*

The story of Hannah is a great example of the power of prayer. Hannah could not bear children for her husband and was constantly teased by her husband's other wife. Whenever there was a holiday, Hannah and her entire family of wives, their children; servants and her husband traveled to the temple to worship.

Instead of Hannah murmuring and complaining, she went to the temple and prayed. God responded to her sacrifice of prayer. He blessed her with three sons!

When we are willing to give a great sacrifice, He responds Greater! He will give us the desires of our hearts when we commit to Him. God gives us power through prayer to have power in prayer!

PRAYER

Dear God, as we position ourselves to receive from You, let us not waiver in consistently seeking Your heart and not Your hand. In Jesus name. Amen."

DAY 19
Self-control.

"But the fruit of the Spirit is love, joy,
peace, patience, kindness, goodness,
faithfulness, gentleness, self-control."
Galatians 5:22-23 *AMP*

Self-control is the ability to have control over one's emotions; it also known as temperance. It is dangerous to be driven by our emotions because they are temporary. When we have a sense of being overwhelmed, or "losing control" we need to stop and take a deep breath in order to regain control.

Self-control/temperance is ONLY one of nine fruit of the Spirit we as Believers should be readily displaying as testament of the Holy Spirit being on the inside of us. As 'fruit inspectors' we must inspect our own before pulling

out the magnifying glass to examine
others.

PRAYER

"Dear Lord, as we are allowing the
Holy Spirit to develop all of our fruit,
please allow Your Mercy to continue to
endure forever. In Jesus name. Amen."

DAY 20
Favor ain't fair.

"You will arise and have compassion
on Zion, for it is time to show favor to
her; the appointed time has come."
Psalm 102:13 *NIV*

The saying, "Favor ain't Fair" is well known. Truthfully, the trial, the testing, and the fire a person goes through in order to walk, live, and embrace favor makes it fair. People think it's not fair because they see what the person has obtained because of favor; not the unfair treatment; unfair warfare; or the loneliness BEFORE the favor.

Noah found favor in the eyes of the Lord. Before favor showed up, remember Noah was laughed at; criticized and lonely. The same favor is available to us today after we are able

to withstand the "unfair" prerequisites.

PRAYER

"Dear Lord, thank You for shining Your

Countenance down upon us. We love

when You "smile" down on us. In

Jesus name. Amen"

DAY 21
I am enough.

"Being confident of this, that he who began a good work in you will carry it on to completion until the day of Christ Jesus." Philippians 1:16 *NIV*

In 2005 I was a in a dark place. I was fired from my job without any idea of what to do next. My bills got behind, and I was robbing Peter to pay Paul! I became so overwhelmed I contemplated suicide. But God!

I got another job and met friend that introduced me to JESUS!!! Once I accepted Christ, I was able to see the Light, and see change on the horizon. I learned how to love myself; flaws and all. I learned God loved me because He created me. I stopped beating myself up and stopped walking and living in fear. STOP! STOP! STOP! I AM ENOUGH! YOU ARE ENOUGH! Once I learned and realized I was enough, life truly got better.

PRAYER

"Dear Lord, when we accepted You, we accepted true love. As we love You teach us how to love ourselves. Help us to value us the way You value us. In Jesus name. Amen."

DAY 22
Resurrection.

"After He had said this, He went to on to tell them, Our friend Lazarus has fallen asleep; but I am going there to wake him up." John 11:11 *NIV*

Lazarus and Jesus were close. Jesus spent plenty of time at his house while Martha and Mary served and waited on Him. After one of Jesus' visits, Lazarus got deathly sick. Martha and Mary sent message after message to notify Jesus of Lazarus' condition; but they didn't get a response or a visit from Jesus.

When Jesus finally showed up, Lazarus had been dead for two days! Martha and Mary were mad; hurt; and disappointed with Jesus. He was telling them what He was going to do about

Lazarus, but they couldn't see or hear past him lying in the grave dead. Instead of Jesus continuing to try to explain Himself, He called Lazarus' name; and Lazarus walked out of the tomb wrapped in his grave clothes on, resurrected from the dead!

The same way Jesus resurrected Lazarus, He resurrect us, our situations, and anything we entrust Him with! Although we may have watched "it" die, if we commend "it" into Jesus' hand's, He can call "it" forth, and "it" will have to LIVE!

PRAYER

"Dear Lord, we know You have ALL power. You are able to resurrect any dead situation. Do it for us Lord. In Jesus name. Amen."

DAY 23
The butterfly effect.

"This means that anyone who belongs to Christ has become a new person. The old life is gone; a new life has begun!" 2 Corinthians 5:17 *NLT*

The butterfly effect is simply what we do today, that will come back to us tomorrow. Even though we may have sown anger, it may show up tomorrow as rage. My grandad would say, "Watch what you do and say to people, because it'll come back on you!" What goes around comes back around just like a boomerang.

We have to be purposeful in what we are sowing. Sow positive things, and we will reap positive things.

PRAYER

"Dear Lord, we understand our transformation will involve what we have sown into our lives and into other's lives. We want to come forth with Your characteristics. In Jesus name. Amen"

DAY 24
Soak in His Presence.

"For since the beginning of the world men have not heard or perceived by the ear, neither have the eye seen, O God, beside thee, what He hath prepared for him that waited for Him."
Isaiah 64:4 *KJV*

Intimacy with God is vital in building a relationship with Him. Getting to know Him becomes very personal. Meditating, or waiting on Him while we worship and pray becomes a priority. Meditating increases our love for God because we put all of our focus on Him.

When we set aside specific time to seek, pray, worship, and meditate with The Lord, we will experience monumental changes in our lives and everyone and everything connected to

it.

PRAYER

"Dear Spirit of the Living God, thank
You for teaching me how to wait in
Your Presence. In Jesus name. Amen."

DAY 25
Wolves in sheep's clothing.

"Watch out for false prophets. They come to you in sheep's clothing, but inwardly they are ferocious wolves."
Matthew 7:15 *NIV*

We have been warned about false prophets and teachers who on the outside seem pure and faithful, but on the inside are full of deceit and evil. These leaders preach the Word in the pulpit but live like dogs succumbing to worldly ways, beyond the pulpit.

We have a responsibility to study and know The Word for ourselves so we will know what is being preached to us is The Word. If the truth of The Word is not being preached, then we must not allow it into our spirits. My pastor says, "Chew the meat, and spit out the bones!"

We can ask God to sharpen our discernment so we can be on guard so as to not allow the things that are not like Him into our spirits.

PRAYER

"Dear God, thank You for Your protection by sharpening my discernment to be able to see the wolves. In Jesus name. Amen."

DAY 26
Rejoice and weep.

"Be happy with those who are happy,
and weep with those who weep."
Romans 12:15 *NLT*

When we attend football or basketball games and our favorite player scores, we cheer, shout, and scream to celebrate them! This is the same type of excitement and celebratory attitude we should have when it comes to our brothers and sisters in Christ. The same God Who blessed them, an bless us because He not a respecter of persons. When we rejoice with others, it makes room for us to be blessed.

When our brothers and sisters in Christ are weeping, we should have enough empathy and compassion to weep with them. Celebrating and empathizing with our brothers and sisters in Christ is small thing, especially when God sacrificed His ONLY sin to save us!

PRAYER

"Dear God, expand our hearts so we may be able to celebrate and empathize with our brothers and sisters in Christ. In Jesus name. Amen."

DAY 27
Shake it off.

"If any household or town refuses to
welcome you or listen to your message,
shake its dust from your feet as you
leave." Matthew 10:14 *NLT*

When people attack us; slander our name; or spread lies about us, we need to understand it is an attack initiated by the enemy. We have to shake it off. No one likes to be rejected or feel unwelcomed, but we have to learn how to shake it off. When we are carrying the Gospel of Jesus Christ, many will not receive us, but there are also many that will.

There are onlookers who are assigned to watch us and report back to the naysayers; the ones who expect us to fail. We have to stop taking things personal when all of it is a part of representing Jesus. We have to stay focused and keep our eyes on the Prize. Shake it off and put it under your feet.

PRAYER

"Dear Lord, toughen our skin so we will remain focused on pleasing You and not man. In Jesus name. Amen."

DAY 28
Bless this house.

"Unless the Lord builds the house, the builders labor in vain."
Psalm 127:1 *NIV*

When building a new house, the foundation is laid first. Once the foundation is secured, the frame is built around the foundation to prepare for the walls and the ceiling.

Just as a house is built to stand against destruction, we must fortify our "houses" with the Word of God to withstand the whiles of the devil. We must present our bodies a living sacrifice, holy and acceptable unto God. God is the Architect and Master Builder. Let Him build our "houses (us)" according to His divine blueprints.

PRAYER

"Dear Lord, we give You permission to lay a sure foundation within us so You may build us to be strong houses of prayer. In Jesus name. Amen."

DAY 29
Serving others.

"After that, He poured water into a basin and began to wash His disciples' feet, drying them with the towel that wrapped around Him." John 13:5 *NIV*

As Jesus's time of death grew closer, He continued to minister and serve. He led by example. He served by example. He lived by example, even though He knew the "church people" were plotting to kill Him.

Sometimes we are put in uncomfortable situations, and we don't understand why. When Jesus washed the disciples' feet it was another example He used to demonstrate a characteristic we should possess. He asked, "Who was the greatest of the two; the one being served, or the one rendering the service?" Jesus not only proved He was about His Father's business; His humility in serving showed it as well.

PRAYER

"Dear Lord, while we serve, help us possess sincerity and to do it with love. In Jesus name. Amen."

DAY 30
Following God's Commandments.

"And Noah did all that the Lord commanded him." Gen. 7:5 *NIV*

God became unpleased with mankind He created. He gave Noah instructions to build an ark. Noah was instructed to take his family; male and female of every animal, because God was going to destroy the earth with rain. Even though everyone thought Noah was crazy, he still obeyed God's instructions. Because of his obedience his family was saved, plus they were the family that replenished the earth after the flood.

Noah's obedience produced many opportunities to be favored by God. We need to be intentional and purposeful in

obeying all the Lord instructs us to do

so favor will find us and open up doors

of opportunity!

PRAYER

"Dear Lord, strengthen and empower us

to obey Your instructions no matter

how pressure is pushing us to disobey.

In Jesus name. Amen."

ABOUT THE AUTHOR

Mrs. Yolanda Simmons

Mrs. Yolanda Johnson-Simmons is a native of Wrightsville, GA. She was raised by the late Charles Johnson and Annie Johnson. Mrs. Simmons attributes her strength of past and present to the example her mother has and continually displays.

Yolanda attended the Johnson County School system where she was actively involved in band, basketball, and cheering. She obtained an associate degree in

Business Administration from Everest University.

Yoland is married to the love of her life, John Simmons. She is the mother of two daughters: one bonus son, and three bonus daughters. She has two grandchildren, of which who have captured her heart! Mrs. Yolanda loves spending time with her family and making memories. She also loves to travel with her family.

Mrs. Simmons is the CEO and Founder of "Yo-Yo's Creations and More" where she brings crafting dreams to reality. Crafting started as a way to earn extra money, now it's her place of peace!

Made in the USA
Columbia, SC
27 July 2023

20812648R00080